Halloween at Merryvale

By

Alice Hale Burnett

CHAPTER I

GETTING READY FOR THE PARTY

"What's Hallowe'en mean, Father?" asked Thomas Brown as the family was seated at breakfast one morning late in October.

"It means the evening before All Saints Day," answered Father Brown.

"Do you remember what fun we had last year, Chuck?" remarked Toad, for Thomas was called "Toad" by his friends, and Charley was known as "Chuck."

"I should say I do," he answered.

The Browns had always lived in the town of Merryvale in a large, white house, set far back from the street, and not far away was the home of Toad's best friend Reddy and his brother Frank nick-named "Fat."

"We had great fun when I was a boy," resumed Father Brown, "for my birthday anniversary falls on Hallowe'en and your grandmother would always have me invite the boys in the neighborhood to a party on that night."

"Oh, I wish mine weren't two days later or I might have a party too," sighed Toad.

"There's no reason, Thomas," said his mother, with a smile, "why you can't celebrate your birthday on Hallowe'en, if you'd like to."

"Oh, Mother, that's fine," cried Toad, jumping up from the table and running around to his mother's place to give her a hearty hug. "You always make things right," he added.

"We'd better ask all the fellows in school today," suggested Chuck, "for Saturday is Hallowe'en."

Toad lost no time when he reached school that morning in giving his invitations to the party and all the boys were glad to accept, for they always had a fine time at Toad's house.

When Saturday morning arrived, Mother Brown sent Toad off to the barn to get some large red apples.

"Be sure they have strong stems," she warned him, "or I shall not be able to use them."

The apples had been packed in barrels with plenty of straw to keep them from freezing, and when Toad reached the barn he pulled out one after another until he thought he had plenty. Just as he was wondering how many trips he would have to make to get all the apples to the house, a face peeped around the doorway.

"Hello, Reddy," laughed Toad, "come on in and help me with these apples. I've got to carry them up to the house," he explained, "they're for the party tonight."

"Couldn't we eat just one now?" asked Reddy, picking up from the floor a shining red apple.

"Hey, not that one," cried Toad, "take one without a stem."

"Huh," protested Reddy, "what difference does that make? I wasn't going to eat the stem."

Toad laughed.

"Mother wants strong stems on them. I don't know why," he explained.

"What's a Hallowe'en party like?" inquired Reddy, seating himself on the top of a potato barrel.

"Fat says," he continued, "that there's always ghosts."

"Aw, who's afraid of baby things like ghosts," jeered Toad.

"Well, I'm not either," protested Reddy. "I knew he was only trying to scare me."

After the boys had carried the apples up to the house Mother Brown looked them over and exclaimed:

"They're just what I want, such fine strong stems."

CHAPTER II

THE FUN BEGINS

At about half past seven o'clock that night the boys who had been invited to the party began to arrive at the Brown's home where they were met at the door by a figure in white. It had queer rabbit ears, made from tying up the corners of a pillow slip that had been placed over its head. The eyes were holes cut in the slip.

The large hall was lighted by many candles set in hollowed-out pumpkins which had queer grinning faces cut in them.

"Wow, but this is spooky," giggled Fat, at which the other boys laughed.

Now the figure in white, which was really Toad, asked the boys to follow him as he led them to Father Brown's study. Here they were met by Chuck, also in white.

"Good evening, Mr. Ghost," greeted Reddy, bowing low.

"How do," nodded the ghost and Chuck could scarcely keep from laughing as he added in a deep voice, "Put on these slips and hurry up," pointing to a pile of them on the floor.

"Oh, I know who you are," laughed Fat, "but I won't tell," and he hastened to scramble into a pillow slip, which he twisted around his head until he got the slits for the eyes in the right place.

"My ears are longer than yours are," boasted Herbie, as he danced about.

"All the better to hear you, my dear," laughed Linn Smith.

As all were now ready, Chuck led the queer looking party of long-eared figures into the library where they were met by Father and Mother Brown dressed in black gowns with tall witches' caps on their heads. There was a large black pot hanging in the fireplace and Mother Brown began to stir something in it with a long iron spoon.

Fat walked directly over to the fireplace and peeped into the pot.

"If ghosts had noses," he sniffed, "I'd say that smelt awfully good."

Father Brown now went about, pinning a number on each boy's back.

"What's that for?" asked Hopie.

"Well, you all look so much alike," laughed Mr. Brown, "that I can't tell you apart. And," after a pause, "there's going to be a prize for this game."

"That's great," shouted Herbie, "hope I get it."

Chuck now left the room, returning a moment later with a huge pumpkin which he placed on a chair in the corner.

"Who's number one?" he asked, at the same time lifting high into the air the stem of the pumpkin, which had been cut off close to its base.

"Keep perfectly still," whispered Chuck as Hopie came toward them.

"I am," announced Hopie Smith from his place before the fire where he had been helping Mother Brown stir the contents of the great black pot.

"Well, hurry and come over here, if you're first," called Toad, "and I'll turn your slip around so you can't see."

"Here's the stem," said Chuck, placing it in Hopie's outstretched hand.

Father Brown now took Hopie by the shoulders and slowly turned him around again and again.

"I believe you've had enough turns to wonder where you are," he said, adding, "now see if you can place the stem on the pumpkin."

Hopie started off, both hands held out before him.

"You musn't feel anything with your hands," called Herbie, "it isn't fair."

"All right," was the answer as he walked straight for the corner where Fat was sitting, watching the fun.

"Keep perfectly still," whispered Chuck in Fat's ear, as Hopie drew near, then as he paused before Fat and placed the stem upon his head the boys broke into shouts of laughter.

"Oh, you pumpkin head," gasped Reddy.

Hopie pulled off his pillow slip and stared in wonder about him, then he too laughed.

"I was so sure I had it on the pumpkin!" he exclaimed.

"Better be careful, Fat," warned Toad, "If mother takes you for a pumpkin she'll put you in a pie."

Numbers two, three and four hadn't much better luck for Herbie stuck the stem on the center table, Chuck on a book stand and Reddy tried very hard to put it into the pot but Mother Brown held out her hand just in time to save it from falling in.

Linn's turn came next.

"Watch me," he said. "I'm going to do it."

"Bet you don't," challenged Reddy.

Then Father Brown gave him a few quick turns and away he started. After taking two or three steps forward he paused, then, stretching out his hands he walked slowly toward the fireplace. When he had reached it he turned about and faced the room.

"Now, I know where I am," he thought, "I'll walk right over to the corner by the door."

"Look," whispered Chuck to Herbie, "he knows where he's going, all right."

Each boy held his breath as Linn drew closer and closer to the chair which held the pumpkin. Then as his knees struck against the edge of it he stopped and placed the stem on the top of the pumpkin.

"Good for you, Linn," cried Toad. "I didn't think you could do it."

"Oh, it was easy," boasted Linn. "The heat of the fire told me where the fireplace was, then when I turned and faced the other way I knew I only had to walk to the left to reach this corner."

"Here's the prize," announced Chuck, stepping up to Linn and handing him a box.

"Hurry up and open it," cried Hopie, "we want to see what's in it." And as the lid came off the box, Linn exclaimed:

"A baseball, just what I've been wanting," and he tossed it up into the air.

"That's as lively as a cricket," commented Herbie, as he caught the ball and bounced it on the floor.

CHAPTER III

THE SWINGING APPLES

Mother Brown now whispered something in Fat's ear and with a broad grin Fat disappeared through the door leading to the kitchen. In another moment he reappeared carrying two large, well-greased pans in his hands. At once the boys all crowded about the fireplace trying to help and in less time than it takes to tell, the taffy that had been boiling in the large pot was poured into the pans and set away to cool.

"By jiminy, I hope it tastes as good as it smells," observed Toad.

"I'm sure it will," replied Mother Brown, with a smile.

"Stand in line," ordered Chuck, "while I tie your hands behind your backs."

"You're not going to spank us, are you?" wailed Fat, making believe to cry.

"No, silly," laughed Chuck, adding, "Everyone take off his slip, now. We need our whole faces to play this game."

Toad, with the help of Father Brown, then placed a long pole so that the ends rested on the top of two bookcases and from it hung many bright red apples, tied on with strings.

"Now," said Chuck, "the fellow who can take one good bite out of an apple without using anything to steady it with, gets a prize."

"Me first," cried Herbie.

"All right," was the reply, "go ahead." And Herbie started.

At first it seemed very easy, but whenever he got ready to take a good bite the apple always slipped away. The boys all laughed as Herbie made one dive after another.

"Ah, have a bite," cried Reddy. "I picked that one out for you."

Herbie then gave the apple a push and stood with his mouth wide open, awaiting the return swing, but instead of getting a bite, the apple landed on his nose.

Fat fairly rolled over with laughter and after a few more attempts Herbie gave up his place to Linn Smith. Then Father Brown took Herbie's apple off the string and, tossing it to him, said:

"Here's the Boobie prize."

Linn had no better luck than Herbie, although he tried his hardest. The apple always bobbed about his head, rolling away just as he thought he had it.

"You're next," called out Toad, as Fat stepped forward toward the apples.

"Good evening," said Fat, bowing low, "I've a very empty feeling, would you like to step inside?"

"Ah, hurry up," shouted Reddy, "I want a turn some time tonight."

"So do I," chimed in Hopie Smith.

Fat grinned. "Don't be in such a hurry; it never pays," he retorted.

Again and again he tried but did no better than the rest. Hopie Smith, who followed, had no success, and then came Reddy's turn. Bending down, he brought his face up under the lower end of the apple and opening his mouth very wide and bringing his teeth together with a quick snap he succeeded in biting a piece out of the apple.

"Dandy," shouted Toad, "he gets the prize," and as he handed the winner a box Reddy opened it and exclaimed:

"Oh, it's a knife, that's great, and I needed one too."

"That's a beauty," declared Herbie, "You're lucky, Red."

CHAPTER IV

THE CANDY PULL

"Don't you think the candy's cold by this time?" whispered Fat to Toad.

"Let's find out," suggested Toad, and the two boys walked over to the table where the pans had been placed to cool. Very gently placing his finger tips upon the candy, Fat exclaimed:

"Oh, it's just right; plenty cool enough to pull."

"Hey, come on, everybody," shouted Toad, "the candy's ready."

"I'll get some butter," offered Chuck, running off to the kitchen, saying as he went: "Wait until it comes; it keeps the candy from sticking."

When he returned the boys all greased their fingers well with butter and set to work pulling the taffy.

"Let's see which one can make his the lightest," suggested Linn. "I used to be pretty good at this work when I was young," he laughed.

"Well, Grandpa, I'll beat you this time," boasted Toad.

"Won't somebody help me out of this?" wailed Herbie, holding up before him two very sticky hands. He had been so anxious to commence pulling his taffy that he had not waited for the butter.

"You're a sad looking sight," laughed Fat. "Why didn't you wait to see how I did it," he chuckled.

"You'd better go and wash it all off," suggested Father, "and make a fresh start, for there's plenty of taffy."

Herbie took his advice.

"Reddy, what was that the teacher said in school the other day about too much candy being bad for little boys?" inquired Chuck from his corner by the fireplace, at which Reddy laughed.

"Come on," he said, "let's see who's taffy's the lightest."

"Yes, everyone hold out his piece," proposed Linn.

"Oh, yours is," admitted Toad as he saw Linn's cream-colored taffy.

"Looks like a lock of Mary Lee's hair," observed Herbie, glancing at Linn's piece.

"You're always talking about her," teased Fat.

"Am not," denied Herbie stoutly, his face turning red.

"Oh, look at the little dear blush," cried Toad in great glee, just dodging the sofa pillow aimed at his head by Herbie.

Hopie, leaning back comfortably against the side of the fireplace, heaved a sigh of contentment.

"Got a tummy ache?" asked Reddy.

"Nope, just enjoying myself," was the answer as he took another bite from his piece of taffy.

"What'll we do next?" inquired Chuck, turning to Father Brown.

"I'm expecting a witch at nine o'clock to tell fortunes," was the reply. "I hope she doesn't disappoint us."

"A witch," shrieked Fat in a high, thin voice, making believe to be very much alarmed. "I hope she won't change me into a snake."

"Oh, you'd make a better turtle—you're so fond of walking slow," laughed Linn.

"She'll turn Herbie into a sleeping Prince, and Mary Lee will be the Princess who kisses him and wakes him up," said Chuck, teasingly, at which all the boys roared with laughter.

As Herbie started off after Chuck a merry chase followed which the other boys enjoyed, at times holding Chuck until Herbie was almost upon him and then letting him go, only to catch Herbie and hold him in turn. Suddenly in the midst of the uproar there came a sharp rap on the door.

"One—two—three."

"Hush," whispered Chuck, "it's the witch."

"Three cheers for Hopie!" shouted all the boys.

CHAPTER V

THE WITCH TELLS FORTUNES

"Come in," invited Father and the boys, standing in a group watching the knob of the door turn slowly. As it opened silently they saw standing on the threshold a little, old woman, all bent over, a long black cape and hood covering her from head to foot. She carried a cane with a crook in it and leaned very heavily upon it as she walked.

Muttering to herself she crossed the room and took a seat by the fire. Her coarse, gray hair fell in straggly locks about her face almost hiding it from view.

Suddenly the lights went out, leaving the room in darkness, save for the firelight.

"Place the pot before me," she ordered, in a high, broken voice, shaking her stick at Fat.

"Yes, Ma'am," said Fat, hurrying to obey.

"She's got Fat scared to death," giggled Toad to Reddy.

From under her cape she now took a small paper bag and poured the contents into the pot before her, then standing up she hobbled around it three times, waving her arms and humming a queer little tune. Soon a dull red light glowed from within the pot, getting brighter and brighter.

"It's magic," whispered Toad to Hopie Smith.

The old witch now sat down again and took from beneath her cape a small pad, a long quill pen and a queer little bottle filled with milky white fluid.

"If you drink any of that you'll get as small as a flea," said Fat in a low voice.

The old witch rapped hard on the floor with her cane.

"Herbie, come forward," she commanded.

"Go ahead," giggled Reddy, giving him a little push and Herbie stepped before the witch.

She did not notice him at first, being very busy writing upon a slip of paper with the quill pen which she dipped into a little bottle. Presently she raised her head and handed him the paper.

"Bend low thine ear," she said, and Herbie obeyed.

"Keep this until I am gone," she added, "then hold it over yonder candle light, for thy fortune is written there."

Each boy was now called in turn and received a slip of paper. Then the old witch arose.

"To those who obey my commands, good luck; to those who disobey, ill fortune," she cried, shaking her stick in the air, and in another moment she had quickly hobbled from the room.

Chuck now turned on the lights and Linn exclaimed:

"Where on earth did she ever come from?"

"Why, witches come out of the air," explained Toad. "They travel on a broomstick."

"Let's see what she wrote on the papers," proposed Hopie Smith.

"Yes," agreed Reddy, "she told me to hold it over the candle light," at which Chuck came forward with a candle that he placed on the center table, holding his slip of paper over the flame. The other boys eagerly gathered about to watch.

Soon the paper got hot and letters began to appear.

"Look, there's an 'a' and two 'e's,' and—and," cried Chuck, "it's quite plain now. I can read it."

"Go on," shouted Reddy, "let's hear it."

Chuck began:

> "If your head will rule your heart,
>   From a cent you'll never part;
>   So tell your heart to rule your head,
>   And all will mourn you when you're dead."

"That means if you're stingy no one will care when you're gone," explained Linn, at which Chuck laughed with the others.

Herbie now held his over the light, and as the letters appeared, he read:

> "Don't always be in too great haste,
>   It often means a dreadful waste;
>   Await your turn and take with ease,
>   The piece you want with fingers greased."

"That's you and the molasses candy," laughed Reddy, adding, "Here's mine:

> "Your hair may be of brilliant hue,
>   But this should never bother you;
>   For when the winter winds blow most,
>   Your head will be as warm as toast."

"That's great," cried Reddy as all the boys laughed.

Fat now held his slip over the flame, and, as the words appeared read slowly:

> "If you should eat a pound of lemons every other day,
>   You'd grow as lean as any pole, for so I've heard folks say;
>   But if, upon the other hand, you keep on eating pie,
>   You'll grow so big and round and tall, you'll almost reach the sky."

"You'd better be careful, Fat, and buy a barrel of lemons," suggested Toad.

"I'll order a wagon-load," grinned Fat.

Hopie now held his paper near the candle, and in a moment read:

> "If you're the lad, to find the coin
>   That's hidden in the flour,
>   You, the highest will enjoy,
>   Of health, and wealth and power."

Toad's turn now came and upon his paper was written:

> "You're very fond of teasing all the girls,
>   And pulling off the ribbons from their curls;
>   But mark my words, these tricks you'll surely rue,
>   For when you're grown, a few they'll play on you."

"That's a good one for you to remember, Toad," laughed the others.

Linn now read:

> "Your mouth may be large, as I've oft heard you say,
>   But your words show a brain that is working;
>   You'll go to the top of the ladder because,
>   You do what you do without shirking."

"The old witch must have liked you, Linn," commented Reddy. "That's the best yet."

CHAPTER VI

BLOWING OUT THE CANDLES

"Let's try to blow out the candles next," suggested Toad, to which the others agreed.

"Bet I win this," boasted Fat, "I've got a lot of wind."

"Reddy ought to win," laughed Chuck, "he's always blowing about what he can do."

A tray with ten candles was now placed upon the table by Toad and the boys got in line while Father Brown lighted the candles. Then, with paper and pencil he stood near at hand to keep the score.

"Only one puff each, remember, so make it a big one," he laughed.

Fat and Herbie, from their places in the line, began at once puffing and blowing.

"Hey, what are you trying to do," called Linn Smith, "start a cyclone?"

"No, we're only practising," was the laughing reply.

"I'll puff, and I'll puff 'till I blow your house in," sang Herbie, adding, "here's where I win."

Hopie Smith, first in line, filled out his chest with all the air it would hold, and stepped forward.

Puff!

"How many?" shouted the others.

"Five," counted Father Brown, "that's a good beginning."

Reddy then gave Fat a poke with his elbow.

"Move up," he urged.

Toad came next and turned around three times for luck and then took a long breath. Puff!

"One, two, three, four," called Father.

"What," cried Toad in surprise, "only four—why, I was sure they would all go out."

Linn came next. Standing upon his toes and holding his hands together high above his head he turned slowly around, then, leaning down he gave a great blow.

"Six," counted Father Brown, "that's the best yet."

"Watch me," cried Chuck, who stood next, and placing his hands upon his hips he started dancing about before the table.

"Ha, look at the funny dancer," shouted Hopie.

Chuck gave a puff and blew out six candles which tied Linn's score.

Fat, who was now next in line, leaned far over. Placing his hands on the floor he lifted his right foot and shook it three times, then standing up he puffed out his cheeks for a mighty blow.

"Look out, you'll bust," warned Herbie.

Puff!

"By jiminy, he did it," cried Toad, "good boy, Fat," as every candle went out.

"Reddy may tie him," suggested Father. "Let's see."

Reddy turned three somersaults for luck and standing before the candles blew with all his strength, and seven went out.

"Fat gets the prize and it's just what he likes most," cried Toad.

"Oh, but I'm glad I came," sighed Fat, as he opened the big box of candy that Toad had handed him.

"Now all be good children," he added, "and I'll give you each a piece."

CHAPTER VII

THE SEARCH FOR THE SILVER COIN

"Shall we try to find the dime in the flour now?" asked Toad of Father Brown, after the boys had all tried some of Fat's candy and found it very much to their liking.

"Fine," agreed Father, "and I'll go to get the pan." When he returned a few moments later he carried a large tin dish-pan in his hands with an inch of flour in the bottom of it.

As Toad thought the floor the best place for this trick, the pan was placed there.

"How do you do it?" asked Reddy, standing with his back to the fire.

"It's very easy," answered Chuck with a grin. "There's a ten cent piece on the bottom of that pan and you've got to pick it up with your lips without using your hands to help."

"I'd have left my hands at home tonight, if I'd known they were to be of so little use," laughed Herbie.

"Oh, you'll need them later on," replied Chuck, "see if you don't."

"Three at a time," called out Father, "in a three minute try to see who can find the dime. Hopie, you, Toad and Fat try first."

The boys screamed with laughter as the queer-looking things bumped about on the table.

Down went all three boys on their knees before the pan of flour and down into the flour went the three faces. Such a puffing and blowing that the flour rose like a white cloud and settled on the heads of the three who were pushing each other about in their efforts to find the money.

"They look like a lot of hungry pigs," laughed Reddy.

"You're not sick, are you Toad?" asked Herbie, "your face looks so pale," at which everyone laughed.

Suddenly Hopie Smith jumped up with the flour falling from his face and the dime held fast between his lips.

"Hurrah; three cheers for Hopie," shouted all the boys.

The pan was now carried out for a supply of fresh flour and a new dime. The three boys were brushed off and soon were watching the others trying to find the dime.

"Say, Reddy, you're an old man," cried Toad, "your hair is turning gray."

"Look out there, Linn," warned Fat, "you'll turn into a pancake if you eat all that flour."

At this Linn laughed, causing a great cloud of flour to rise from the pan.

"Chuck's digging for sil——" but before Hopie could finish Reddy stood up, his dancing blue eyes shining like two stars. Between his lips he held the dime.

"Good for you, Red," shouted Toad, "I knew you'd win it."

CHAPTER VIII

THE WONDERFUL PIE

Mother Brown now appeared in the doorway.

"Won't you come into the dining room?" she requested, and the boys lost no time in accepting the invitation.

"That means something to eat," whispered Herbie. "Wonder what it'll be."

As the boys entered the dining room they started with surprise, for there, hanging over the table, was the huge grinning face of a jack-o-lantern.

"Well," exclaimed Fat, "what a sweet face!" which brought a round of laughter from the others.

In the center of the table was a large paper pie and seven ribbons came from under the crust, each of them having a card on the end. A plate of paper snap-crackers of bright colors and the fancy yellow paper napkin at each place gave the table a gay look.

"What a funny pie," laughed Hopie. "What's inside?"

"Each one find the card with his name on it. Then we'll all pull together," directed Chuck, "and find out."

"Here's yours, Fat," called out Linn.

"You're over here, by me, Reddy," announced Toad.

"The fun's going to begin in a minute," cried Herbie. "Come on, Hopie, here's yours."

"Everyone ready now," cried Toad as each one held on to his own ribbon. "Now, one, two, three, pull," and, with a tearing of paper out came the contents of the pie.

Huge wiggly spiders, toads that hopped about the table, mice that looked real enough to frighten any girl, long striped paper snakes and giant grasshoppers were on the ends of those ribbons.

The boys screamed with laughter as the queer-looking things hopped, rolled and bumped about on the table.

"Look at what I've got," shrieked Hopie, holding an ugly looking spider up to view.

"If that was real I'll bet you wouldn't be within ten feet of it," said Fat.

"I'm going to scare our girl into fits with this mouse," laughed Herbie. "She'll just take one look at it then hop up on a chair; and won't she be mad when she finds out it isn't real?"

"Say, fellows, watch this frog jump," cried Fat, winding up a green and yellow one made of tin.

"Bet mine can beat it," boasted Reddy. "Let's race them."

"Thought yours could hop further than my little Heinie, didn't you?" teased Fat a minute later after his frog had won.

"Well, you wait until I get mine oiled up," warned Reddy, "and we'll try it again."

When the boys pulled the snappers, the gay paper hats caused great merriment, Fat having a baby cap with long strings which he tied under his chin.

"Ah, here comes the ice cream!" exclaimed Herbie. "Look at the funny figures it's in," he added, as a large platter, holding many odd little shapes, was placed before Toad.

"Youngest first," announced Toad. "What do you choose, Hopie?"

"I'll take, let's see; guess I'll have a pumpkin," finally decided Hopie and a yellow ice-cream pumpkin was placed before him.

"You're next, Reddy," said Chuck.

"Am not; Herbie's younger than I am," protested Reddy.

"I'll take the rabbit," laughed Herbie. "I like chocolate and vanilla best."

Reddy now chose a pink and white wind mill, Chuck a pony.

"Don't I wish it was real," he said.

"Well, the turtle looks like it might taste pretty good," said Fat, and then it was Linn's turn.

"It doesn't seem fair for you to be last, Toad, when you ought to have come after Reddy," remarked Linn.

"Oh, well, it's my party, so I have to be last," was the answer.

"Well," agreed Linn, "if that's so I'll have the ship."

"Oh, good," cried Toad, "that leaves the engine for me and I wanted it more than anything else."

"This turtle makes better ice cream than he would soup," grinned Fat as he took another spoonfull.

"I'm eating my rabbit's ears first," chirped Herbie.

"Well, I'm eating the smoke from my engine, first," Toad chimed in.

"Here's the cake, you'll have to cut it, Toad," Linn informed him, "for it's bad luck to let any one else cut a birthday cake for you."

It was covered with white icing and ablaze with candles.

"Now watch the candles go out," and Toad gave a great puff. "All over," he declared, laughing, "now I'll cut the cake."

"There is a piece of silver in it, Thomas," said his mother, "and the one who gets it will be the lucky one in life, and a thimble for the one who is going to be a bachelor."

At this the boys urged Toad to hurry and when the cake had been cut and passed around each boy looked his piece over carefully.

"Hurrah, I've got the money," shouted Hopie, holding up a bright dime so all could see.

"And I've got the thimble," wailed Chuck. "Now I'll have to sew on all my own buttons."

"Hopie's lucky all right; he won the money in the flour, too," observed Herbie.

It was now growing late so the boys, much against their will, found their hats and bade good-night to Father and Mother Brown.

"We've had a fine time, Toad," said Fat, "hope you have another birthday next year."

"I'm very sorry to have to do it," announced Linn, grasping Toad and turning him over his knee, "but you must have nine spanks and one for good luck."

"Why didn't we think of it before?" agreed the others, helping to hold Toad until each one had his turn.

"Well, I ought to be good for a year, now," laughed Toad, after he managed to get away. "Wait 'till it's your turn, Linn, won't I give you some good ones?"

"Good-night," responded Linn, "we've had a dandy time."

"You bet we have," echoed all the others.

"Good-bye, good-bye," called Chuck and Toad, standing in the doorway as the boys disappeared in the darkness.

THE MERRYVALE GIRLS

By ALICE HALE BURNETT

Four delightful books for the smaller girls, each a complete story in itself, describing in simple language the interesting experiences of Beth, Mary and Jerry, three little maids of Merryvale.

BETH'S GARDEN PARTY

The three girls take part in a very formal little affair on the lawn of Beth's home. Each of the guests receives a present in the shape of a downy white kitten. The drive home in Beth's pony cart furnishes a few exciting moments, but Patsy bravely comes to the rescue.

A DAY AT THE COUNTY FAIR

The girls are taken to the fair in a motor, but a slight delay occurs on the way. How they finally arrived at the fair ground and their amusing experiences are most entertainingly told.

GERALDINE'S BIRTHDAY SURPRISE

Geraldine, whom of course we know better as Jerry, plays the part of hostess to her many friends, although it must be admitted that her guests knew of the affair before she did. A jolly evening is spent by the girls which is shared in by some of our young Merryvale boy friends.